HOPE
for the Hurting
BIBLE STUDY
TONY EVANS

Lifeway Press®
Nashville, Tennessee

EDITORIAL TEAM

Heather Hair
Writer

Reid Patton
Content Editor

Jennifer Siao
Production Editor

Jon Rodda
Art Director

Joel Polk
Manager, Adult Short-Term Publishing

Brian Daniel
Director, Adult Ministry Publishing

ISBN: 978-1-0877-5477-2
Item number: 005835700

Dewey decimal classification: 152.1

Subject heading: PAIN / SUFFERING / JOY AND SORROW

My deepest thanks go to Mrs. Heather Hair for her skills and insights in collaboration on this manuscript.

Unless indicated otherwise, Scripture quotations are taken from the New American Standard Bible®, Copyright © 1960, 1962, 1963, 1968, 1971, 1972, 1973, 1975, 1977, 1995, 2020 by The Lockman Foundation. Used by permission. *(www.lockman.org)*

To order additional copies of this resource, write to Lifeway Resources Customer Service; One Lifeway Plaza; Nashville, TN 37234; fax 615-251-5933; call toll free 800-458-2772; order online at *lifeway.com;* email *orderentry@lifeway.com.*

Printed in the United States of America

Adult Ministry Publishing • Lifeway Resources • One Lifeway Plaza • Nashville, TN 37234

Contents

About the Author

Dr. Tony Evans is the founder and senior pastor of Oak Cliff Bible Fellowship in Dallas, founder and president of The Urban Alternative, former chaplain of the NBA's Dallas Mavericks, and author of over 100 books, booklets, and Bible studies. The first African American to earn a doctorate of theology from Dallas Theological Seminary, he has been named one of the twelve most effective preachers in the English-speaking world by Baylor University. Dr. Evans holds the honor of writing and publishing the first full-Bible commentary and study Bible by an African American.

His radio broadcast, The Alternative with Dr. Tony Evans, can be heard on more than 1,400 US outlets daily and in more than 130 countries.

Dr. Evans launched the Tony Evans Training Center in 2017, an online learning platform providing quality seminary-style courses for a fraction of the cost to any person in any place. The goal is to increase Bible literacy not only in lay people but also in those Christian leaders who cannot afford nor find the time for formal ongoing education.

Dr. Tony Evans was married to his late wife, Lois, for nearly fifty years. They are the proud parents of four, grandparents of thirteen and great-grandparents of three.

For more information, visit TonyEvans.org.

How to Get the Most from this Study

This Bible study book includes six weeks of
content for group and personal study.

GROUP SESSIONS

Regardless of what day of the week your group meets, each week of content
begins with the group session. Each group session uses the following format to
facilitate meaningful interaction among group members, with God's Word, and
with the teaching of Dr. Evans.

START. This page includes questions to get the conversation started and
to introduce the video teaching.

WATCH. This page includes key points from Dr. Evans's teaching, along with
blanks for taking notes as participants watch the video.

DISCUSS. This page includes questions and statements that guide the group
to respond to Dr. Evans's video teaching and to relevant Bible passages.

PERSONAL STUDY

Each week provides three days of Bible study and learning activities for individual
engagement between group sessions: "Hit the Streets" and two Bible studies.

HIT THE STREETS. This section highlights practical steps for taking the week's
teaching and putting it into practice.

BIBLE STUDIES. These personal studies revisit stories, Scriptures, and themes
introduced in the videos in order to understand and apply them on a personal level.

Tips for Leading
a Small Group

Follow these guidelines to prepare for each group session.

PRAYERFULLY PREPARE

REVIEW. Review the weekly material and group questions ahead of time.

PRAY. Be intentional about praying for each person in the group.

Ask the Holy Spirit to work through you and the group discussion as you point to Jesus each week through God's Word.

MINIMIZE DISTRACTIONS

Create a comfortable environment. If group members are uncomfortable, they'll be distracted and therefore not engaged in the group experience. Plan ahead by considering details like seating, temperature, lighting, food and drink, surrounding noise, and general cleanliness.

At best, thoughtfulness and hospitality show guests and group members they're welcome and valued in whatever environment you choose to gather. At worst, people may never notice your effort, but they're also not distracted. Do everything in your ability to help people focus on what's most important: connecting with God, with the Bible, and with one another.

INCLUDE OTHERS

Your goal is to foster a community in which people are welcome just as they are but encouraged to grow spiritually. Always be aware of opportunities to include any people who visit the group and to invite new people to join your group.

An inexpensive way to make first-time guests feel welcome or to invite someone to get involved is to give them their own copies of this Bible-study book.

ENCOURAGE DISCUSSION
A good small-group experience has the following characteristics.

EVERYONE PARTICIPATES. Encourage everyone to ask questions, share responses, or read aloud.

NO ONE DOMINATES—NOT EVEN THE LEADER. Be sure that your time speaking as a leader takes up less than half of your time together as a group. Politely guide discussion if anyone dominates.

NOBODY IS RUSHED THROUGH QUESTIONS. Don't feel that a moment of silence is a bad thing. People often need time to think about their responses to questions they've just heard or to gain courage to share what God is stirring in their hearts.

INPUT IS AFFIRMED AND FOLLOWED UP. Make sure you point out something true or helpful in a response. Don't just move on. Build community with follow-up questions, asking how other people have experienced similar things or how a truth has shaped their understanding of God and the Scripture you're studying. People are less likely to speak up if they fear that you don't actually want to hear their answers or that you're looking for only a certain answer.

GOD AND HIS WORD ARE CENTRAL. Opinions and experiences can be helpful, but God has given us the truth. Trust God's Word to be the authority and God's Spirit to work in people's lives. You can't change anyone, but God can. Continually point people to the Word and to active steps of faith.

KEEP CONNECTING
Think of ways to connect with group members during the week.

Participation during the group session is always improved when members spend time connecting with one another outside the group sessions. The more people are comfortable with and involved in one another's lives, the more they'll look forward to being together. When people move beyond being friendly to truly being friends who form a community, they come to each session eager to engage instead of merely attending.

Encourage group members with thoughts, commitments, or questions from the session by connecting through emails, texts and social media.

When possible, build deeper friendships by planning or spontaneously inviting group members to join you outside your regularly scheduled group time for meals, fun activities, or projects around your home, church or community.

Week 1

COMING TO THE COMFORTER

Start

Welcome to Group Session 1.

What shapes a person's view of his or her painful experiences in life?

How do upbringing, past experiences, expectations, and coping skills impact the healing process when painful scenarios pop up?

Imagine a Christmas tree with stacks of presents placed at its base. Examine each carefully wrapped present in your mind. You're likely not visualizing identically shaped and sized gifts because Christmas presents come in all shapes and sizes. Similarly, each person's pain, trauma, and triggers are unique to them. Your scars, scares, and challenges are unique to you. There is not a one-size-fits-all pain moment for all people. Neither is there a one-size-fits-all solution to the hurts we feel.

Everyone experiences pain differently. Some of us face it well. Some of us try to deny it. Others, even, succumb to its crushing weight, which only leads to more pain through the compounding consequences of additional poor personal choices. Unfortunately, many people miss the opportunities for growth that pain provides. The purpose of this Bible study is to help you face life's difficulties with dignity and come out stronger because of it.

Invite someone to pray, then watch the video teaching.

Watch

Follow along as you watch video Session 1.

Discuss

Use the following questions to discuss the video teaching.

The passage we're going to discuss is an anchor passage for trying times.

Read this passage together and then discuss the following questions.

For we do not want you to be unaware, brethren, of our affliction which came to us in Asia, that we were burdened excessively, beyond our strength, so that we despaired even of life; indeed, we had the sentence of death within ourselves so that we would not trust in ourselves, but in God who raises the dead; who delivered us from so great a peril of death, and will deliver us, He on whom we have set our hope. And He will yet deliver us, you also joining in helping us through your prayers, so that thanks may be given by many persons on our behalf for the favor bestowed on us through the prayers of many.
2 CORINTHIANS 1:8-11

Have you ever heard the statement "God won't give you more than you can handle"? Why is this statement untrue and unhelpful?

We've all heard the statement that God won't put more on you than you can bear. No one wants to be the bearer of bad news, but this statement is untrue at best and unhelpful at worst. God often puts more on us than we can bear when he's trying to strip us of ourselves and lead us to depend on Him in our weakness. If we never experienced more than we could bear, there would never be a reason to depend on God.

Have you experienced a time when God put more on you than you felt you could bear? If so, what did you learn through that experience?

What are some reasons you believe God may allow us to struggle beyond what we feel individually able to solve or fix?

In the video, Dr. Evans talks about the season in the Evans home where they lost eight family members to death over a period of just two years. This season of crushing was more than they could bear on their own. He talks about how there are times in our lives when God is the only One remaining with strength to lean on because all human strength is gone. This is actually a good place to be— depending on the goodness of God and the faithfulness of others. In this passage, Paul described that the ultimate goal of our affliction is thankfulness for the favor that would be brought to us through the prayers of many.

What does it look like in practical terms to set your hope on God in the midst of a hopeless situation?

What power comes when people come together to pray in one accord? When have you felt the benefits of personal prayer?

Share a time you came to know God's favor personally when you faced a hopeless scenario, and what was the result?

PRAYER

Lord, in times of trials and difficulties, it is easy to lose hope and lose heart. But You desire to produce new life and new gratitude through these difficult times. Help us not to give in to the despondency and despair, but rather help us to look to You with a spirit of expectation that Your favor will see us through this painful season. In Jesus' name, amen.

Hit the Streets

PUSHING THROUGH

When a person exercises, he or she will often look to something outside of themselves to distract them during the pain. This distraction helps them to keep going and push through. God doesn't want to just distract you in the pains of life, but He wants to comfort you. That is even better. His comfort provides a way for you to push through the challenges of hurt and loss, while also maximizing the opportunity for personal growth and development.

Below are three key passages, and a space for you to write a personal summary of each, to keep your eyes on when you are going through a painful season.

These things I have spoken to you, so that in Me you may have peace. In the world you have tribulation, but take courage; I have overcome the world.
JOHN 16:33

Personal Summary:

For just as the sufferings of Christ are ours in abundance,
so also our comfort is abundant through Christ.
2 CORINTHIANS 1:5

Personal Summary:

Naked I came from my mother's womb, and naked
I shall return there. The LORD gave and the LORD has
taken away. Blessed be the name of the LORD.
JOB 1:21

Personal Summary:

SEEKING COMFORT

If you live in Texas or the surrounding states, you will remember—like me—the terrible freeze we all went through in the early part of 2021. I had COVID-19 at the time with moderate symptoms. So, not only was I struggling to heal from the virus, I was also cold. The whole house was cold. The power grid had been hit so hard that many thousands lost power. In fact, nearly 200 people lost their lives during this horrific winter storm.

In order to keep warm, I had to use a number of blankets and comforters. My point might be obvious but in order for the comforters to do what they were created to do—keep me warm during the coldest winter I had ever known—I had to go grab them and cover myself with them. If the comforters were stacked in the closet or in a basket, they would do no good. I had to make the decision to go get the comforter and shelter under them in order to benefit from them.

Similarly, God offers us comfort in our difficulties and pain. But He doesn't force His comfort on us. We need to seek Him out and grab hold of His truths and presence to gain access to His comfort. In other words, God's comfort is abundant but not automatic. We must participate with Him in the process of pain in order to realize the powerful nature of His comfort. The Scriptures teach that God is a God of comfort.

Read the following verses and pull out the phrases on "comfort" in each one. Write them below the verse:

Blessed be the God and Father of our Lord Jesus Christ,
the Father of mercies and God of all comfort.
2 CORINTHIANS 1:3

Comfort phrase:

> Who comforts us in all our affliction so that we will be able
> to comfort those who are in any affliction with the comfort
> with which we ourselves are comforted by God.
> **2 CORINTHIANS 1:4**

Comfort phrase:

> For just as the sufferings of Christ are ours in abundance,
> so also our comfort is abundant through Christ.
> **2 CORINTHIANS 1:5**

Comfort phrase:

God's comfort comes to us in the midst of suffering and affliction. If it were a hot summer day in Texas, I wouldn't have needed the comforters I rested beneath during that disastrous winter storm. I needed the comforters because of the cold. Similarly, we experience God's comfort when we choose to look to Him for comfort instead of to deny the difficulties we are facing.

In what ways does contemporary Christianity and even secular psychology teach people to deny the difficulties they are facing and put on a facade?

What eventually happens when a person denies or ignores the pain in his or her life?

Acknowledge the pain in your heart doesn't make you less spiritual. You aren't more mature because you put your chin up and pretend that life's blows don't really get to you. Stuffing your emotions so that you can tell others you are "blessed by the Best" only creates a ticking time bomb in your spirit which will eventually blow. We heal from pain by acknowledging it.

No one ever healed by ignoring a wound rather than treating it. Wounds heal when they are washed, cleansed, treated, and kept clean. Similarly, pain in our hearts needs to be acknowledged and addressed in order to heal.

Identify one painful area in your life which you may have been glossing over. Why have you chosen not to face it?

Why is acknowledging your pain necessary for receiving the comfort God has supplied?

Why do we fool ourselves into thinking denying or hiding our pain will be more comforting than admitting it?

How can we encourage one other to be more transparent about our wounds so that we can receive the healing and comfort we need?

The Greek word for "comforter" used in the verses we examined on the previous page shares a root word with a term Jesus used to describe the Holy Spirit in John 14:16. Here Jesus said "I will ask the Father, and He will give you another *Helper*, so that He may be with you forever."

Thus, in every affliction, trouble, hurt, pain, distress, or difficulty that you may be facing, there is a Comforter. There is a blanket of blessing, if you will choose to grab it. Now, it's possible to spend so much time in a cold room complaining about the cold all the while not choosing to pull the comforter up over you. The comforter is there. You're just more focused on the temperature in the room.

Your focus affects what your experience.

Read Romans 8:28-29.

And we know that God causes all things to work together for good to those who love God, to those who are called according to His purpose. For those whom He foreknew, He also predestined to become conformed to the image of His Son, so that He would be the firstborn among many brothers and sisters..
ROMANS 8:28-29

What perspective do these verses give you concerning God's purpose for your pain?

Describe some characteristics of a person "conformed to the image of" Jesus Christ.

How might that relationship with Jesus shape his or her experience with pain?

Pray about your pain, troubles and triggers. Do you view them through the lens of God's purpose? Are you actively seeking to be conformed to the image of Jesus Christ more so than desiring a life of ease?

PRAYER

Spend some time in prayer asking God to align your heart and spirit with His purposes, and to enable you to be more authentic and aware of the personal traumas of your life that you need to acknowledge, address, and look to God for comfort in.

Bible Study 2
LIFE LOOPS

The promises of God's Word have never been a guarantee from pain and trouble. Rather they are promises to experience God in pain. Oftentimes, God does manifest His victory on our behalf by removing the challenge or bringing us through, but not until He has developed us through it. Being able to develop through our pain is a mark of spiritual maturity. It proves that when we are pressed we find comfort from our Comforter.

List some qualities of spiritual and emotional maturity..

Which of those qualities do you feel would be difficult to possess and maintain during painful times?

What is one quality of emotional and spiritual maturity you would like to strengthen in order to sustain you during hard times in life?

In fact, God will often allow us to remain in a painful situation until we are ready to be delivered from it. He does this in order that we might strengthen our spiritual maturity. When you or I don't learn the lessons we need to learn, it positions us in a life loop—a cyclical pattern of loss and pain. Until you break the cycle and seek God's grace for healing and growth, you'll be caught in a loop of self-doubt and limitation. Life loops are those times when we find ourselves being forced to learn the same lessons over and over again.

How can we find purpose in our pain and move beyond the life loop?

Understanding the purpose behind your pain requires accepting the sovereignty of God. God's sovereignty is His total control over all of life. It means that nothing happens to you unless it passes through His fingers first. In every circumstance, either God has caused it or He has allowed it. If He caused or allowed it, He has a reason for it. When you grasp that core spiritual truth, you can move past the "why me" or the "I wish I would have" or "If only I" or "If only He" thoughts and begin to acknowledge the fallout of the pain you are facing. You can shift your thinking in order to look for the important lesson at hand.

Is there an important life lesson that you feel may have been put on a "loop" in your life so that you are facing multiple opportunities to learn it?

Why do you feel this lesson is on a "loop"?

I often compare the life loop lessons we experience to taking a test in school. If you fail a test in school, the teacher will often ask you to retake it because the goal of teaching is to help you understand information and the only way the teacher knows that you understand the information is through passing the test. Similarly, God gives us tests in our own lives that center on aspects of wisdom, spiritual growth, and maturity. When we fail to learn these lessons, we'll be asked to take the same test again. Life loops happen to us in order to awaken our hearts to the critical need for spiritual growth.

When have you learned a tough lesson after many attempts at trying to learn it? Describe how you felt once you broke through and applied life's wisdom to your lesson.

One of the key traits people learn when going through a life lesson is humility. As you are probably aware, humility is a critical component of wisdom and essential for the Christian life. God intentionally opposes the proud (Ps. 138:6; Prov. 3:34; 29:23). That means, when you operate from position of pride or self-service, God will not get behind what you are doing. His Word tells us time and time again that pride comes from sin.

Pain removes pride from our hearts because it reveals our humanity. It reveals our need to honor and love others, and to not think more highly of ourselves than we ought. Pain topples the towers of pride erected in our souls. And while this may be unpleasant to go through, the outcomes, if you cooperate with the lessons of pain and loss, will be worth it. You'll find yourself living with greater levels of peace, contentment, and joy when you live a life devoid of pride.

Read the following verses and summarize their key points in your own words.

For the LORD is exalted,
Yet He looks after the lowly,
But He knows the haughty from afar.
PSALM 138:6

Summary:

"Behold, I am against you, arrogant one,"
Declares the Lord GOD of armies,
"For your day has come,
The time when I will punish you."
JEREMIAH 50:31

Summary:

The Lord GOD has sworn by Himself, the LORD God of armies has declared: "I loathe the arrogance of Jacob, And detest his citadels; Therefore I will give up the city and all it contains."
AMOS 6:8

Summary:

For the LORD of armies will have a day of reckoning
Against everyone who is arrogant and haughty,
And against everyone who is lifted up,
That he may be brought low.
ISAIAH 2:12

Summary:

What do these verses communicate as a whole?

PRAYER

Pray and ask God to reveal to you what lessons you need to learn from the painful life loops you have experienced. Let God know you want to break free from the cyclical lessons you've faced. Ask Him to place people and situations into your life to help you learn and apply what you need to in order to develop spiritual maturity at a deeper level than you've previously experienced.

Week 2

DISCOVERING THE TREASURE WITHIN

Start

Welcome to Group Session 2.

Let's pause for a moment to review from last session about coming to the Comforter. When pain hits, we have a tendency to retract and retreat. However, the purpose in our pain can only be found when we place ourselves under the cover of the Comforter.

What is one big lesson you learned last session?

This session will focus on how our brokenness can lead to breakthrough.

What does it mean to be spiritually or emotionally broken?

How can brokenness lead to something beneficial in a person's life?

The good stuff in life is often found below the surface. If you enjoy peanuts, you know that no one gets excited about a the shell. In fact, the shell is often discarded as fast as possible. That's because we want the treasure inside. But in order to get to the good, the shell has to be to be ripped off and removed.

God has a treasure in you and He wants you to uncover it. Because of this, He will sometimes allow things to come into your life that may be painful, inconvenient, or difficult to bear. But He does this so that the "life of Christ" may be made increasingly more manifest in all you do and say. Brokenness is often the road to breakthrough.

Invite someone to pray, then watch the video teaching.

Watch

Follow along as you watch video Session 2.

Discuss

Use the following questions to discuss the video teaching.

We've all seen a butterfly fluttering as it dances from flower to flower. We are amazed at how magnificent butterflies are, but they didn't start out that way. They started out as caterpillars. They started out crawling around slowly. They were not beautiful. They were plain. And yet the caterpillar was the beautiful and magnificent butterfly. It just had to be formed within.

Like the caterpillar turning into the butterfly, spiritual transformation is a process. List some steps or practices that lead to spiritual transformation.

God is in the transformation business. God is able to bring about an even greater metamorphosis in our hearts and souls if we let Him have His way in us. He can take what is plain or even ugly and transform it into something beautiful.

Why do you think pain or loss is often used as a way of transforming people's lives?

Why might it be more difficult to spiritually grow during times of ease than in times of challenge?

What are some things a person can do to stay stuck in a cocoon and refuse to cooperate with the transformation of spiritual development?

Every time God allows you to be perplexed, confused, and go through a difficult situation, it is pain with a purpose. It is brokenness leading to a breakthrough.

When has working through a painful season in life given you new-found purpose and clarity?

Why would God use the painful and bad things in our life for good? What does God's willingness to transform our pain into treasure tell us about His character?

God is into remodeling. Perhaps you've had something remodeled in your home, and you've had to tear stuff up so that your home could be updated and made new. Like remodeling a home, remodeling our lives can feel messy and painful. But if you will look at this from the standpoint of a treasure, it will help. You've got something in you that God wants to bring to the forefront and remove from the background, and that is the treasure of Jesus Christ. To find that treasure, God has to break through our self-sufficiency.

Why would God use the painful and bad things in our life for good? What does God's willingness to transform our pain into treasure tell us about His character?

PRAYER

Lord, You are in the remodeling business. You take that which is slow and unproductive, and You turn it into something amazing and productive. But oftentimes this is a painful situation of transformation. Help us to learn about You and the way You work throughout this time with others in studying Your Word. We want to learn so that we can grow more fully and transform into that which You have destined us to be. In Jesus' name, amen.

Hit the Streets

BREAKING THE BANK

If you've ever owned a piggy bank, you know how hard it is to get the money out once you have put it in. It is fun to keep putting money into the piggy bank knowing that you are storing up treasures for your future. But if you are like me, when it came time to turn it over and dump it out, you probably grew impatient.

Sometimes we shake and shake and shake the piggy bank upside down trying to get the coins inside, only to discover that the only way to truly access them is through breaking the piggy bank open. Most piggy banks designed when I was growing up were made that way. There was no real way to access the bounty of your savings but through brokenness.

Similarly, God uses brokenness in our own lives to release the inner treasure He has within us. When we don't comply, we will often wind up experiencing shaking after shaking . We go along with this until we eventually realize that cooperating with the breaking God is carrying out will get us more quickly to the treasure He has in store. Here are three ways you can cooperate more fully when life's losses and pain add up:

1. SPEAK GOD'S TRUTH into your situation. Look at His Word related to the pain you are experiencing and write reminders of His truth for you to see and say throughout your day.

> **What truth from God's Word do you need to apply to your present pain and struggles?**

2. SEEK GOD'S COUNSEL. Rather than live in a confused state in the midst of calamity, ask God to reveal the purpose for the pain you are experiencing. Seek Him and His answer in prayer.

When has God shown you His purpose in your pain? What confidence should that give us that He will do it again?

3. THANK GOD for what He is producing in you and through you. This is not the same as thanking Him for the pain you are going through. Rather, you are thanking Him and believing that He cares for you and is with you.

Write out a prayer to God thanking Him for His work in your life.

If you will commit to do these three things regularly and with a sincere heart, you will be able to witness God show up in a way you never anticipated. He does not want you to quit when things get tough. He wants you to grow.

Bible Study 1

SHAKE OR BAKE

Like the illustration of the piggy bank features on the previous pages, God has placed a treasure in you and me—in what the Bible calls "earthen vessels." Like a kid shaking a piggy bank He wants the treasure inside of us to come out. Sometimes He has to flip us over and shake us. Other times He has to turn us around and let things rattle a bit inside. Then certain occasions require us to be broken to release the treasure within.

Breaking usually takes place when we refuse to cooperate with the shaking. One way we frequently refuse is through keeping ourselves so distracted and numbed from our pain that we fail to face it in order to let it do its work in us.

List some common ways people try to distract themselves from facing the pain in their lives?

What are some routine outcomes of those distractions?

Review Paul's teaching on earthen vessels.

But we have this treasure in earthen containers, so that the extraordinary greatness of the power will be of God and not from ourselves; we are afflicted in every way, but not crushed; perplexed, but not despairing; persecuted, but not abandoned; struck down, but not destroyed; always carrying around in the body the dying of Jesus, so that the life of Jesus may also be revealed in our body.

2 CORINTHIANS 4:7-10

According to this passage, what is the desired outcome of affliction?

What does it mean to be afflicted, but not crushed?

List four character qualities that become evident in a person's life when "the life of Jesus" is "revealed in our body"?

- _____

- _____

- _____

- _____

Although we'd like to, we can't avoid the pain and jump to the part where Jesus will be manifest in our body. It doesn't work that way. When God permits the troubles we face, we must face them. God redeems negative experiences to grant us a deeper level of intimacy with Him. If we trust God, Jesus will never be more real to us than in those times when life does not seem to be working out.

Why might Jesus feel more dear to you in times of trouble than in times of blessing and prospering?

Paul intentionally used the term "earthen vessel" in this passage. In biblical days, the term "earthen vessel" would be referring to a clay pot or jar. Inside of that pot would often be placed something extremely valuable. By using this as an example, Paul was pointing out that what is inside of us—our eternal spirit—is far more valuable than what contains us. Pain shifts our focus from the external to the internal. Taking a God-centered perspective on our pain allows us to make the most of our difficulties and hurts in life so that we benefit from them rather than simply endure them.

What happens in our spiritual lives when we choose not to participate with the pain but rather to wallow in it, or succumb to it?

What are some things that must take place in our spiritual lives for pain to produce something positive?

I realize that it would seem much easier for all of us if we could just cut any and all painful circumstances from our lives. We could move from celebration to celebration. But life doesn't work that way. In fact, just the opposite is true. Thankfully God takes our pain and uses it to grow us.

The way we are to experience the fullness of life itself is through the death of the flesh and its desires. And that can be a painful process. Whether that means the death of wrong desires, sinful passions, misplaced trust, illicit ideas or even the need for security, predictability, and stability—death must take place before true life comes forth.

When you and I are seeking to unwrap the treasure of the experiential knowledge of God by looking at the face of Christ, we must be willing to identify with Christ. God will often allow circumstances in our lives that are painful in order to help us see Jesus more authentically.

What does it mean to "identify with Christ"?

What is one step you can take to more fully identify with Christ in whatever season you find yourself in?

Jesus came that we may know God more fully and in a more personal way. So, if you want to unwrap the treasure of God in you, just look to Jesus Christ. When you look to Christ and identify with Him, you get all the wisdom and knowledge there is to have because all of that is found in Jesus. As you draw nearer to Jesus during the hurt and pains of this life, you will experience God truly and fully.

PRAYER

Spend some time praying about what you may need to allow God to break in you so that you will surrender to a greater degree to His power. Ask God to soften your heart as you go through this study, as well as to help you maintain a level of commitment to fully benefit from what we are going to learn together. Take time to pray for the other individuals going through the study with you, if you are going through it as a group. Ask God to heal their pain and develop them into spiritually mature kingdom followers of Jesus Christ.

Bible Study 2
REFINED

Problems can help us put to death, or remove, something within us that needs to be removed. This can be compared to how the heat of an oven is designed to kill the bacteria which could harm us in raw meat. While the meat is hot in the oven, it isn't done until the internal portions have been cooked thoroughly. Some people will stick a knife or a fork in the meat to test it. Others might put a meat thermometer in it to let them know when it's done. If the meat is not done on the inside, it can be dangerous to whomever eats it.

Now, if the meat could talk it would remind you that it is very hot and uncomfortable in the oven. It might remind you that 350 degrees doesn't feel all that good. But none of that talk and complaining would matter to you because as the person cooking the meat, it's your job to make sure it is safe for those who consume it. Your purposes overrule that of the meat itself. Similarly, God's purposes for our lives rank higher than our own. He has a reason for the trials and difficulties we face. It is through the heat of hurt and suffering that we are often refined when the bacteria of sin is put to death.

How might pain be a catalyst for removing harmful or destructive behavior and thoughts from a person's life?

It if isn't handled wisely, how can pain lead to a larger degree of harmful behavior and thoughts in a person's life?

While you and I cannot control the things that happen to us, we can control how we respond. Only you get to choose whether or not life's hurts lead to more harm or to healing and growth. Oftentimes, God uses life's difficulties to wake us up to things in our life that we need to get rid of. Though the pain we experience may not come from personal sin, pain has a way of teaching us about our struggles with sin by bringing the most important things in life into focus.

Whatever it is that is keeping you from following God must go. It must be removed so that you stand before Him stripped, honest, and authentic. Like old paint or varnish on a piece of furniture, there are seasons when our souls need to be stripped of that which is covering up the beauty of the treasure within.

What are some approaches you have used in the past which helped you treasure Christ and reject sin patterns of thought and behavior?

In what ways did changing those thoughts or behaviors help to improve your life?

Healing from life's hurts involves learning the lesson the pain was allowed to teach you. In order to learn from the lessons of pain, you need to turn to God's Word to discover what He wants you to know in the wilderness seasons of life. Paul wrote in 2 Corinthians 4:13 that while you are going through the difficulties you are facing, to check our experiences against the truths of Scripture then allow those truths to permeate our lives and speak louder than our pain.

At the urging of the psalmist, David, allow your pain to deepen your thirst for the Lord (Ps. 42). Let your mouth and your belief say the same thing, and let them both agree with what God says is true. In other words, speak God's Word to your situation.

Read 2 Corinthians 4:13 and answer the following questions.

> But having the same spirit of faith, according to
> what is written, "I BELIEVED, THEREFORE I SPOKE,"
> we also believe, therefore we also speak.
> **2 CORINTHIANS 4:13**

What is first required in order to believe God's Word?

How much time do you intentionally spend studying or getting to know what God says in His Word?

How might getting to know what God says in His Word equip you to weather your pain with grace and confidence.?

If you really want to overcome the defeating impact pain has had in your life, or the cyclical nature of life's hurts impeding your progress and deflating your emotions, you need to pursue God through His Word. Then, you need to speak the truth He reveals to you. Our pain refines our hearts and gives us a testimony of God's grace and goodness in our pain.

When you are going through something that you don't want to go through, encourage yourself with truth. Paul and David experienced pain as righteous men. Their relationship with the Lord enabled them to grow their faith through their pain. They had faith in God's Word, therefore they spoke of His goodness and His refining treasure.

Who do you know who has experienced spiritual growth through pain? What could you learn form their belief?

Read 2 Corinthians 4:16-18.

Therefore we do not lose heart, but though our outer person is decaying, yet our inner person is being renewed day by day. For our momentary, light affliction is producing for us an eternal weight of glory far beyond all comparison, while we look not at the things which are seen, but at the things which are not seen; for the things which are seen are temporal, but the things which are not seen are eternal.

2 CORINTHIANS 4:16-18

Based on this passage, what is the intended result of affliction and pain?

What is the pathway to this intended result?

What does it mean to "lose heart?" How do we keep from losing heart while waiting for healing?

Paul used terms like "momentary" and "light" when describing pain. This is coming from a man who acknowledged he was at the point of wanting to give up entirely. But what he is encouraging us to remember is that if the suffering seems long or if it seems heavy and burdensome, it is because we are looking at what we can see. We are fixating too fully on the temporal reality we are in right now. And if all you see is what you see, you do not see all there is to be seen.

Paul isn't saying that we should deny the reality of our hurt or circumstances. But he is saying we should shift our focus. How you view what you are facing will change how you feel about what you are facing. When you place your pain and your hurt in the grid of God's grace and His glory, you will discover the peace that passes understanding.

PRAYER

Pray for the wisdom and internal discipline to shift your focus, especially when times are tough. Pray for the power to look beyond what you can see. God will give you the grace you need when you focus your eyes on Him. Ask Him for His greater grace which will lift you above the defeating emotions produced by life's hurts.

Week 3

THE GREATNESS
OF GRACE

Start

Welcome to Group Session 3.

Last session we talked about discovering the treasure within. How did this session help you reconsider how God uses our pain to make us more like Christ?

This session we will be talking about the grace of God we experience during our trials and tribulations.

How would you define the word *grace*?

Share an example of where you have seen God's grace working in someone's life that has made a positive impact on others.

Oftentimes we seek to provide our own understanding of what "grace" is in our lives by attempting to provide only that which God can supply. Grace is God's work in our lives. We receive the benefits when we choose to surrender to His plan and cooperate with His provision of grace to us and through us. To receive grace requires trust. It requires letting go of our perception of personal control. But when you do, you will discover that God's grace gives you life, strength, power, and peace.

Invite someone to pray, then watch the video teaching.

Watch

Follow along as you watch video Session 3.

Discuss

Use the following questions to discuss the video teaching.

Diamonds are admired for their beauty and brilliance, but diamonds are only formed by immense pressure in a dark environment. We all want the diamond, but we don't want to go through the process that builds the diamond. Yet from God's point of view, that process is one of the ways we experience God's grace.

Read Paul's words together.

> Because of the extraordinary greatness of the revelations, for this reason, to keep me from exalting myself, there was given to me a thorn in the flesh, a messenger of Satan to torment me—to keep me from exalting myself! Concerning this I pleaded the Lord three times that it might leave me. And He has said to me, "My grace is sufficient for you, for power is perfected in weakness." Most gladly, therefore, I will rather boast about my weaknesses, so that the power of Christ may dwell in me.
> **2 CORINTHIANS 12:7-10**

How might our pain actually be an act of God's grace to us?

When grace gets mixed with pain, Paul says it produces power." Pain in and of itself does not produce power. In fact, when pain is not mixed with grace or surrender to God's will, it can produce even greater pain.

What are some things unredeemed pain produces in a person's life?

Paul tells us that God's power is perfected when we are weak. And yet our culture teaches us that only the strong survive. Satan tries to deceive us by pushing a difference agenda that keeps us working and striving rather than embracing our weakness and the grace that comes with it.

Describe some ways Satan seeks to insert a counter-argument to the truth that God's power is perfected in our weaknesses.

Why does it often take repeated exposure to "thorns" in our lives before we will humble ourselves before God and accept His strength?

Can you share a time in your life when you learned to rely on God's strength while you were weak? What did you learn through this?

God loves to use weakness as an opportunity to show His strength. He wants you to become content with your weakness. What does contentment mean? It means to be at ease where you are because you are looking to God to meet you in that space.

Why is contentment so hard to come by in our culture?

How does experiencing grace lead to contentment?

PRAYER

Lord, we praise You knowing that nothing has come into our lives that did not first pass through Your hands. We praise You because You know how to carry us through difficult times. We praise You because You will supply all our needs in order to face the pain we're feeling. We look to You in hope and anticipation for Your presence in our lives. In Jesus' name, amen.

Hit the Streets
SUPPORT SYSTEM

When challenges or difficulties in life appear, they require a concerted focus on God and His sovereignty to overcome. At times this can be hard to do because your mind and emotions are so consumed by what you are dealing with and feeling. That's why it is good to have people come alongside of you to help you refocus on God. Sometimes that is your family. Other times it could be your church, or a pastor. And then other times it might be helpful material, including Bible studies like this one. Before we get into the study content, let's review three practical steps to take to ensure you are surrounded with the support system you need when life hands you a painful loss.

1. IDENTIFY the people in your life who know the words to say to lift you up, or who can point you in the direction of hope and God's unfailing word. If you feel comfortable, let them know you are struggling and you welcome their advice.

Who are these people in your life?

2. ASK GOD to reveal wisdom to you by directing you to messages online or in books that speak to the specific hurt you are facing. Trust Him to guide you to the resources He knows will comfort you and help you to redirect your thoughts onto Him.

What is a resource that has helped you in the past? Who might you ask to direct you to faithful biblical resources?

3. MAKE A LIST of things which bring you joy when times are tough. It might be good to do this when you are not in the season of loss itself, that way you can reference it when difficult times come. Use this list to help you focus on anything which will refocus your thoughts onto God and His will for your life to experience the fullness of life which Jesus Christ died so that you could live.

List out those things that bring you joy and help you see the goodness of God.

If you will commit to doing these three things in the periods of life when loss hits you hard, you will have set up a support system around you to keep you on track for healing. Look to God to guide you. Don't dismiss Him because the pain becomes too much to bear. Instead of blaming Him, seek to understand why He has allowed what He has and what He is trying to develop in you as a result of it.

Bible Study 1

PLATFORM OR PRIDE

What our culture calls trauma, setbacks, disappointments, difficulties, pain, and trials, God redeems and repurposes for His purpose. Seeing our challenges from a kingdom perspective helps us grow from them rather than be defeated by them. No lesson was ever learned in a vacuum. Personal development, similar to physical strength and skill development, benefits from the pain of the process.

Your perspective on pain matters more than the pain itself. When seen from a healthy, truth-based perspective, pain and difficulties produce an awareness of the gift of God's grace that we may not have received otherwise.

Read 2 Corinthians 12:7,9 and answer the following questions.

> Because of the extraordinary greatness of the revelations, for this reason, to keep me from exalting myself, there was given me a thorn in the flesh, a messenger of Satan to torment me—to keep me from exalting myself! [...] And He has said to me, "My grace is sufficient for you, for power is perfected in weakness." Most gladly, therefore, I will rather boast about my weaknesses, so that the power of Christ may dwell in me.
> **2 CORINTHIANS 12:7,9**

Give an example of what you might consider to be a "thorn in the flesh"

How does human weakness magnify the strength of God's power?

What have your own limitations taught you about relying on God for spiritual power?

Humility seems to be a lost virtue in today's culture of so-called influencers, rampant narcissism, self-promotion and celebrity-ism. Satan gains a lot of power over God's people when the allure of platform and pride enslave them. As an apostle Paul had specific revelation from God. This gift of spiritual insight could easily become a snare if it led to increased pride. God taught Paul to rely on His power by afflicting Paul with "thorn in the flesh" God allowed to afflict him.

What are some ways our contemporary culture feeds narcissistic tendencies, even in Christian circles?

Why are personal pride and unhealthy self-concern such spiritually corrosive habits?

How do our social media habits reinforce vanity and pride.

The idols of personal elitism and harmful pride has infiltrated our Christian leaders, podcasters, and social-media influencers. Dopamine highs for gaining likes have often turned "Christian ministry" into nothing more than "platform building." The body of Christ is being torn apart from within by endless self-promotion and consumerism that is barely distinct from the culture. Scripture is clear that Satan feasts on unchecked pride, yet the contemporary Christian culture seems numb to his advances.

Consider John's warning:

> For all that is in the world, the lust of the flesh and
> the lust of the eyes and the boastful pride of life, is
> not from the Father, but is from the world.
> **1 JOHN 2:16**

Describe the difference between honoring God with our lives, personal platforms and our conversations contrasted with honoring ourselves?

Paul's temptation to pride came through increased insight into spiritual matters. Many Christians have pride today that comes through increased popularity within the various silos of Christian culture. It doesn't matter what the source of the pride is, if a person is to truly live out his or her purpose, the pride needs to be recognized for what it is: a tool of the devil. And it needs to be rooted out by God. Unfortunately for many of us, that rooting out requires pain.

Read Proverbs 26:12

> Do you see a person wise in his own eyes?
> There is more hope for a fool than for him.
> **PROVERBS 26:12**

On a scale of 0-10 (with 10 being the most), how wise are you (look at your personal decisions to inform your answer) in your own eyes?

0   1   2   3   4   5   6   7   8   9   10

Read Proverbs 27:2,.

> "Let another praise you, and not your own mouth;
> A stranger, and not your own lips."

On a scale of 0-10 (with 10 being the most), how does social media promote a culture of praising ourselves (even if couched in a "God taught me this …" scenario)?

0   1   2   3   4   5   6   7   8   9   10

What areas of your life do you need to ask for God's grace to release you of your reliance on other people's approval, praise, and admiration?

PRAYER

Close out today's session by being authentic in your personal struggle with self-promotion or image. Pray about how to let go of the need for personal control in your life. Ask God to infuse your heart with a heartfelt humility which will enable you to truly grasp the power of His grace. As you pray through these things, write down any changes God brings to your mind that He wants you to make in your future conversations, social media posting and/or viewing, and priorities of your time.

Bible Study 2

THE GOAL OF GRACE

Have you ever admired a pearl? Or either worn or purchased a pearl necklace for someone you loved? Pearls are exquisitely beautiful.

And while much mystery remains around exactly how pearls are made, we do know a few things. First of all, they come from oysters. For the pearl to form, a irritant enters the oyster. Because the oyster is not able to remove the irritation, it has been designed with a coping mechanism—the increased secretion of nacre. Nacre is an composite material which naturally lines the inner shell of oysters and other mollusks. On its own, the nacre isn't valuable. But when the nacre begins to surround a grain of sand or grit, it develops into a pearl.

The pearl didn't start out as a pearl. The pearl started out as an irritant. It started out as something which was entirely unwelcomed, undesired and unexpected. Pearls are formed out of protection. They are literally formed out of a need to soothe pain. The iridescent coating helps the oyster live with what it could never get rid of on its own. What began as irritating and unwelcome becomes magnificent and invaluable.

When you are in the middle of that which is causing you pain and hurt, it's easy to fixate on the problem. But if you will learn how to cope with the problem through the grace God has given you, you can participate in the birthing of beauty from within.

Read James 1:2-4:

> Consider it all joy, my brothers and sisters, when you encounter various trials, knowing that the testing of your faith produces endurance. And let endurance have its perfect result, so that you may be perfect and complete, lacking in nothing.

Similar to the irritant inside the pearl, how can a "trial" produce endurance and wholeness in a person's life?

How can God's grace transform our irritants into endurance?

God has a purpose for the pain you are experiencing in your life. You must believe that truth in order to benefit from the pain He has allowed in your life. If you truly want to know how to cope with the pain and hurt in your life, then you need to turn to God and ask Him why He has allowed it. You need to discern from Him what it is He is wanting you to use as tools to cope with it. He may or may not remove it. But you have a choice in how you respond to it.

Why is it important to turn to God for wisdom when we face life's hurts?

Read the following verses and write in your own words some of God's purposes for the hurt we experience in life.

> As Jesus passed by, He saw a man who had been blind from birth. And His disciples asked Him, "Rabbi, who sinned, this man or his parents, that he would be born blind?" Jesus answered, "It was neither that this man sinned, nor his parents; but it was so that the works of God might be displayed in him."
> **JOHN 9:1-3**

God's purpose:

Before I was afflicted I went astray, but now I keep Your word.
PSALM 119:67

God's purpose:

Beloved, do not be surprised at the fiery ordeal among you,
which comes upon you for your testing, as though something
strange thing were happening to you; but to the degree that you
share the sufferings of Christ, keep on rejoicing, so that at the
revelation of His glory you may also rejoice and be overjoyed.
1 PETER 4:12-13

God's purpose:

All discipline seems not to be pleasant, but painful;
yet to those who have been trained by it, afterward
it yields the peaceful fruit of righteousness.
HEBREWS 12:11

God's purpose:

Blessed are those who mourn,
for they will be comforted.
MATTHEW 5:4

God's purpose:

When Paul suffered from what he called a "thorn in the flesh," God told Paul that His grace was sufficient for him. He explained that spiritual power becomes perfected through weakness. He didn't remove the thorn. He didn't even heal the hurt. The torment remained just like the grain of sand or grit inside an oyster. But what God did do is reveal to Paul the path forward through the pain. Like the oyster coating the sand, God told Paul to coat his thorn with His grace.

The word "grace" is a term many of us use but few have truly maximized. Sure, we've experienced grace in salvation but we have not experienced the power of grace in our everyday lives. Grace is God's divine provision to us in need. Grace is the undeserved favor God bestows upon us. In other words, grace is the inexhaustible supply of God's goodness. And while we often want the thorns of life pulled out and the pain to cease, God says there are times and seasons when the grace we need to get through pain will reveal the sufficiency of His power within us.

What is the difference between knowing about grace intellectually and experiencing it personally?

God will never run out of grace. He has enough for you. He has enough for me. And over the last year, I have learned that when life gets tough and you don't know how you will bear it on your own, God's grace gives us the power to make it through.

Thorns, when accompanied by His grace, are designed to work for us—not against us. In this way, the thorn literally becomes an asset even though it once felt like a liability. But once you mix that thorn with God's grace, that grain of sand becomes a priceless pearl.

PRAYER

End your time today by praying for the thorns you or those you know are currently experiencing. Pray that God will grant you the grace you need to cover your thorns and turn them into a means to experience His power and purpose in spite of your weakness.

Week 4

HEALING THROUGH HUMILITY

Start

Welcome to Group Session 4.

Last session, we learned about how God takes our pain, covers it with grace, and turns it into something powerful and purposeful. When have you experienced this?

This session we're going to talk about the vital connection between healing and humility. Having the right regard for our own limitations will bring us to a place where we are ready to receive God's healing.

How do people respond when life feels hopeless?

How might these responses keep us from reaching a place of peace?

Many of the circumstances that make us feel hopeless are the things we can't overcome with our own effort. Yet, despite knowing this, we still grind our gears and spin our wheels trying to topple life's obstacles rather than turning to God in humility. We seek our own solutions rather than turning to the One who can do all things. It's often our lack of humility that keeps us from reaching to God.

In the story we are about to explore in this study, a woman simply touched the tassels on Jesus' robe and received healing. Christ's power was accessed through her act of humility.

Invite someone to pray, then watch the video teaching.

Watch

Follow along as you watch video Session 4.

Discuss

Use the following questions to discuss the video teaching.

Many people today are living lives of desperation. They are hemorrhaging. They are hemorrhaging with pain, disappointments, unfulfilled dreams, depression, anger, resentment, or bitterness. The longer we struggle, the harder it becomes to hold on.

Read Mark 5:25-34 together.

What drove this woman to approach Jesus? How did she model humility in her approach?

The lady we will be studying in this week's session spent a considerable amount of time sick and bleeding. She suffered from physical ailments for years. Often we are able to cope with our hurts because we know they're short term, however, when seasons of struggle or loss go on indefinitely, our hope begins to fly out the window.

Why do you think prolonged suffering eats away at hope and strength more than temporary suffering?

What are some spiritual practices that a person needs to keep the faith in the midst of prolonged seasons of pain?

Can you share a Bible verse that helps you when you are dealing with pain that seems to just go on and on?

God wants to intervene in our pain so that He establishes a brand new relationship. He's not interested in just a religious association. He wants us to be up tight and close. Unfortunately though, many people draw more distant from God when pain goes on in their lives for an extended period of time. But God wants you, like the woman in the biblical example, to draw close to Him.

How often is our failure to reach out to God caused by our lack of humility?

What are some of the feelings and thoughts people have which causes them to draw away from God rather than close to Him during times of pain and loss?

What are some preemptive measures that can be put in place during seasons that are good to help a person draw closer to God and not want to push away when things get bad?

When we fail to reach out to God in our sorrow and hurt, we are communicating that we've got everything handled. We don't fail to reach out to God because of a lack of time or resources, but rather we don't reach out from an abundance of pride. The woman in the Scriptures was not proud. She humbly approached Jesus and received what she knew only He could offer. May our faith be like hers—humble.

PRAYER

Lord, help us to have the faith to draw close to You. We do not want to shrink back in faith, but we find ourselves tempted to do so when the pain in our heart feels like it is too much to bear. Help us to reach out to You even when we question what is going on. Honor our faith for praying. Honor the faith it takes us to look to You when we are tempted to look the other way. In Jesus' name, amen.

Hit the Streets

YOKE UP

When life gets hard we all face the temptation to quit. At first we may face our struggles head on thinking we possess the strength to deal with it. We may even feel like we are full of faith. Yet when the troubles of life ebb on day after day, or week after week, or even year after year—our strength and resolve ebbs away too. It can happen to anyone.

This is why it is so important to keep your eyes focused on Jesus. Keep your heart focused on living in a state of humility, being willing to bend down low enough to touch the hem of His robe. You need Jesus' strength the most. His power will push you through. Abiding in Him yokes you to the One who gives rest to the weary and might to the weak. Let's look at three ways you can cultivate your relationship with Jesus Christ.

1. SPEND REGULAR TIME IN GOD'S WORD. We read that Jesus is the Word of God revealed to us in human form. He is the direct reflection of God Himself. If you want to know Him better, get to know and understand God's Word better.

> **How often are you spending time with God in His Word? How can you make the most out of that time?**

2. SPEAK WITH CHRIST. Prayer isn't always about bowing your head and closing your eyes. You can talk with Jesus at any time. Just direct your thoughts to Him—your questions, concerns, hurts. Nothing is too hard for Him to hear. You can be honest. In fact, He already knows the truth of what you are feeling so telling Him won't be a surprise.

What are you learning from God through prayer?

3. LISTEN FOR HIS RESPONSE and look for His presence in your life. Abiding with Jesus simply means to "hang out" with Him. I'm sure you've never hung out with your friends all alone. In order to hang out with them, you need to be connected with them in some form or fashion. The same is true for abiding in Jesus. Listen for what He is saying to you. Quiet yourself and create space to be alone with God. He is with you. But life becomes so busy that you may need to declutter your life to create the room to recognize God's nearness.

What is a distraction you could remove from your life to more clearly hear from Jesus?

There are times in life that you just can't make it on your own. You need Jesus. You need His help, His presence, and His hope. Make Jesus a priority every day so that when life gets hard, which it does at some point for everyone, you will already have the powerful presence of Jesus so near to you that you will know how to access His ongoing strength.

Bible Study 1

HUMILITY AND ETERNITY

One of the ways to manage personal pain and to heal from hurt is by keeping an eternal perspective. Our lives may feel like they go on forever and the days seem long when we suffer, but our time on earth is a blip on the calendar called eternity. Living with an eternal perspective enables us to manage pain more effectively because we see it as temporary and grow in a posture of humility toward our never-ending God. We learn to view it in a way that enables us to learn from it and grow because of it.

Read these verses and answer the questions that follow:

Before the mountains were born
Or You gave birth to the earth and the world,
Even from everlasting to everlasting, You are God.
PSALM 90:2

He has made everything appropriate in its time. He has also set eternity in their heart, without the possibility that mankind will find out the work which God has done from the beginning even to the end.
ECCLESIASTES 3:11

What does it mean for God to be "from everlasting to everlasting?"

Though we aren't eternal, what does it mean to have eternity in our hearts?

While God has set eternity in our hearts, we are simultaneously limited in our grasp of what that means. Our finiteness keeps us from fully understanding the work which God has done from the beginning to the end. Yet despite these limitations, we can comprehend enough about God and His eternal nature to heal from life's hurts.

How should knowing that God is eternal shape your approach to dealing with temporary pain?

Eternity never ends. And while this can be a hard concept to grasp, grasping it is essential. I want you to consider eternity through this illustration. If there was a way to empty out the largest body of water in the world, the Pacific Ocean, we would be left with an empty abyss bigger than we could even fathom. If somehow we pulled a drain-plug on the Pacific, the remaining hole would be huge.

Now, imagine trying to fill that hole up with sand so much so that you wind up making a pile of it that reaches as high as some of the highest mountains in the world. For example, we filmed Bible study in Alaska, home to the tallest mountain in North America, Denali, which soars over 20,000 feet above sea level. So if we filled the ocean's hole with enough sand to reach as high as Denali, we'd have a considerable amount of sand.

But what does this have to do with eternity? If we were to then have a bird take one grain of sand from that sandpile in the ocean which stretches as high as Denali, and that bird was to deliver each grain of sand to a new location before flying back to get another—how long would it take to complete this task? Probably more time than we can even count. Whatever the length of time, it will only be a drop in the bucket in eternity.

Why should God's eternal nature help us cultivate humility?

Many people stay stuck in the pain of the present because they lack an eternal perspective. God has set eternity in our hearts because He knows that is where we are headed. The time we spend on earth develops and conforms us into the likeness of Jesus Christ. These acts of faith require the humility to recognize that God's way is better than our own because His perspective extends far beyond our own. Our response to life's pains and challenges enables us to invest in future gains.

Read these words from Jesus and use them to further your understanding of eternity.

> Do not store up for yourselves treasures on earth, where moth and rust destroy, and where thieves break in and steal. But store up for yourselves treasures in heaven, where neither moth nor rust destroys, and where thieves do not break in or steal; for where your treasure is, there your heart will be also.
> **MATTHEW 6:19-21**

What can happen to treasures on earth?

1.

2.

What can happen to treasures in eternity?

1.

2.

How does having your heart where your treasure is impact your everyday decisions and responses to life's pain?

A.   **Treasures on earth:**

B.   **Treasures in heaven:**

One of the initial steps to healing life's hurts is to align your heart with an eternal perspective. Once you do that, you will look to Christ for His help based on His Word. You will set aside your own methods and approaches to healing, and rely on His. This requires humility. As we take in God's Word, we let go of our pride.

How has reading God's Word given you a growing sense of humility?

Faith is for the humble in heart, and Jesus told us that mountains can be moved by faith (Mark 11:23). Mountains are often symbolic of insurmountable difficulties. And sometimes the biggest mountains we need to move exist in our own minds. They are what we call "limiting beliefs." Other ways to describe these mindset mountains are "doubt," "cynicism," "regret," and disillusionment." Faith can move these mindset mountains. But faith only becomes real in the context of an eternal perspective. If you fixate too much on the here and now you will fall prey to these mindset mountains because you will miss what God is preparing you for in the hereafter.

Why is it important to focus on God's eternal perspective when using tools of faith to address life's difficulties and hurts?

PRAYER

As we close this study, spend some time praying about your thoughts. Ask God to adjust your thinking to that of viewing all of life from His eternal kingdom perspective. Ask Him to reveal to you where you have been short-sighted so that you can increase your faith in His Word. God's Word reveals wisdom for life but that wisdom is couched in eternity. While you pray, repent of any limiting beliefs you may have, and share with God how you want to honor Him and His Word through aligning your thoughts to His truths.

Bible Study 2
THE POWER TO HEAL

Early in 2021, I came down with COVID-19. I couldn't have picked a worse time to get it. The day I got diagnosed followed a couple of days of pretty awful symptoms. The now infamous Texas Freeze hit in full force, closing roads and shutting down power grids the day before. So, not only was I sitting home alone suffering through the symptoms of COVID, I lived with the awareness that if anything went wrong, getting to a hospital would be difficult. Ice covered the roads for several days making them impassable. Even if I called for emergency help, there would be no guarantee they could reach me.

If you're familiar with my books or sermons, you have likely heard that I don't cook. Needless to say, that was a very long week as I struggled to recover on limited food, limited warmth and little-to-no company. Occasionally a family member would stop by with some prepared food and place it inside the front door. When you are sick, other things can pile up to contribute to more than just the sickness itself. It might be loneliness from isolation, financial pressure, or any sort of thing. The woman we read about in Luke 8 reflects this fully. Not only was she suffering from an issue of blood for twelve years, but she was now considered an outcast in society. On top of that, the doctors had drained her finances dry.

Let's look at her life's narrative a little more closely for context:

Read the following verses and answer the questions:

A woman who had a hemorrhage for twelve years and had endured much at the hands of many physicians, and had spent all that she had and was not helped at all, but instead had become worse.
MARK 8:25-26

And a woman who had suffered a chronic flow of blood for twelve years, and could not be healed by anyone.
LUKE 8:43

Now if a woman has a discharge of her blood many days, not at the period of her menstrual impurity, or if she has a discharge beyond that period, for all the days of her impure discharge she shall continue as though in her menstrual impurity; she is unclean.
LEVITICUS 15:25

What were some of the practical implications for being ritually "unclean" in the way that Leviticus describes?

What emotions must that woman have felt when she "could not be healed by anyone" and "had spent all that she had and was not helped at all"?

How do you imagine she felt about herself as a result of being ostracized, or even perhaps bullied, by a culture who considered her "unclean"?

For a Jewish person to be "unclean" meant the person could not be touched. She could not enter the temple to worship God. She was an outcast. So not only did she have to face a life of physical, financial and spiritual pain, she was also alone, outcast, and surviving without much hope at all.

A few years ago, this woman's story may have seemed distant to us. It may have felt like a narrative no one could identify with, in our country at least, in any shape or form. But the onset of a global pandemic led to isolation and quarantining for countless people—this woman's emotional life may feel much more relevant than ever before.

Many families experienced what it was like to have a loved one fall sick and be unable to visit them. Many were prohibited from checking in on their elderly relatives in long-term care facilities. If you fell sick yourself, like I did, then you know what being sick in isolation felt like. People may have dropped off medication or food to your door, but the lack of personal comfort that comes through the freedom of human interaction was jarring. As a result, emotional and spiritual issues increased alongside physical issues.

Even if you did not become sick, you still can relate to the issue of life closing down all around you. The woman we read about in the Gospels doesn't seem so far-fetched to many of us anymore.

In what ways have you recently struggled or experienced other people's struggles? What residual pain or hurt may need to be addressed or healed?

The lady we read about in the Gospels had run out of options. She had lost all hope. But that's when she heard about this man named Jesus who was coming to her town. If you are familiar with the story, then you know she didn't come to Him the normal way people do. She didn't introduce herself or start a conversation. Rather, she did all she could do with the strength that she had. She came up behind him, low to the ground and touched the fringe of his clothes.

Luke's rendering of her story tells us that when she touched His garment, she was immediately healed. Her hemorrhaging stopped (v. 43). But, if we look closer at her story by reading what Matthew had to say, we will discover that it wasn't the garment which did it. Matthew describes what happened like this,

> A woman who had been suffering from a hemorrhage for twelve years came up behind Him, and touched the border of His cloak; for she was saying to herself, "If I only touch His cloak, I will get well."
> **MATTHEW 9:20-21**

She was talking to herself. She was encouraging herself. Despite her isolation and the rest of the entire known world to her at that point having given up on her, she had not yet given up herself. She clung to what she believed and approached Jesus with complete humility. Her humility put her in a position to receive healing from Jesus. The problem many of us face is that we lack the humility to seek the healing we need.

Why is it important to fully believe in Christ and His healing power in your life?

Why does this belief require some humility on our part?

How do you identify with this woman? What are some of the emotions she may have had or her motivations that you can relate to and why?

How might you demonstrate greater humility toward Christ and His power to heal your hurt and pain?

PRAYER

Pray right now and ask Jesus to reveal His power in your life on a deeper level. Ask for His healing balm of grace and love to flow over you. Seek His Word and His ways in order to discover the liberating effects of faith. Honor God through your faith-filled actions and words, then allow His healing power to infuse you with all you need to live free from the shackles of unhealed pain. Jesus has the power to heal you completely from whatever it is that troubles your heart. Turn to Him, bow low before Him in humility and believe He is able to do all that you need to live whole.

Week 5

COME GET
YOUR REST

Start

Welcome to Group Session 5.

Last session focused on the need for humility to handle our pain. How would you describe the connection between humility and healing?

Walking through seasons of difficulty and pain can be exhausting. This session we're going to think about the rest that is available to us through Jesus.

Name common causes of burn-out and depression in our culture.

Why is so hard to live in a perpetual state of rest, peace or contentment?

Each of us has the opportunity to carry our burdens to the Lord. Jesus says, "Come to me," in the powerful passage we are going to study in this week's lesson (Matt. 11:28-30). He doesn't say to wait inside the confines of your own pain for Him to show up and take it all away.

When you carry your burdens to Christ, He will give you rest. He will remove the pain causing you to remain awake when you should be asleep. He will cart off the load piling high in your soul and limiting your kingdom effectiveness. He will do all of this but you have to do something first. You have to choose to carry your burdens to Christ.

Invite someone to pray, then watch the video teaching.

Watch

Follow along as you watch video Session 5.

Discuss

Use the following questions to discuss the video teaching.

Rest is essential to heal from pain. The mental and emotional strain of struggling with life's pain can take a toll on anyone. Rest rejuvenates a soul and brings a fresh perspective when things feel down.

Read Matthew 11:20-30 together.

List all that Jesus tells us to do in this passage?

How does hearing this invitation from Jesus comfort you?

Rest has been given to us through Jesus Christ. He tells us to come to Him if we are feeling weak and weary and He will give us rest. We will look at that more fully in this week's lesson, but for now, let's discuss some of the benefits and ways we can seek rest in the middle of life's pain.

What are some things you do that bring you a feeling of rest?

Identify some small changes you could make to your schedule and commitments which could provide you greater rest when you need it.

What is something you could do to lighten the load and provide rest for a struggling friend?

Rest is such an underrated value in our busy culture today. We run ourselves ragged chasing after each new thing. But rest is important for the body, spirit, and the soul. Rest is being offered for free by Jesus Christ to unload the trash, the accumulation of toxic input, and the realities that are weighing you down. Jesus says, "I will give you rest." He invites you to come to him. He's available."

If Jesus is truly available, why don't we come to Him? What are we missing out on by refusing to come to Him?

How does refusing to come to Jesus actually prolong our struggles and pain?

Jesus is available to give you rest. You just need to take your burdens to Him. He's not going to pry them from your hands. You have to willingly surrender your burdens to Him. Cast your cares on Him. He really does care for you.

PRAYER

Lord, we bring you the pain we're feeling right now. The hopelessness and weariness that is in our hearts is weighing us down. We cannot do this on our own. Will You help us? Will You lighten this stress load we're carrying? Take our worry and replace it with Your calm. Take our fear and give us Your peace. Heal that which is causing us, and those we love, so much pain. In Jesus' name, amen.

Hit the Streets
LOCK-IN TO REST

When many of us were younger, churches would often have what are called "lock-ins." A "lock-in" is where the youth of the church, chaperoned by adults, would celebrate together with games and other fun activities all night long. There would be a lot of laughter, joking, and energy exerted through all-night basketball games or other things. These are a lot of fun. But when the next day shows up, you've got a lot of tired youth and adults on your hands. Despite our desire to have fun, human bodies require rest to function well.

Rest is also a critical part of healing emotional pain, trauma, and loss. Many people do not realize how much trouble it takes to process pain. The energy stores used for getting through a day are spent on frayed nerves and grief. A person can find themselves constantly worn out and drained. When a person lacks good rest, the body shuts down. The mind shuts down. Thoughts are harder to focus. Life in general becomes more difficult to get through.

Jesus offers us rest, and we're going to look at His rest more fully in this week's lesson. Let's also look at three things we can do to help our body, mind, and spirit rest in seasons of loss.

1. SPEND TIME IN GOD'S CREATION. This may mean just going outside and putting your feet in the grass. God has given us a way of connecting with Him through His creation. If we take the time to slow down and experience His creation, we can find additional rest and restoration.

Where are those places that you find most restful?

2. CLEAR YOUR SCHEDULE OF CLUTTER. This will look different to everyone but it could mean reducing the amount of texting or phone calls you take part in. Or it could mean limiting your time on social media or watching the news. Do some self-reflection to help identify what is clutter and what is essential in your life.

If your profession and commitments allow, what would it look like to leave your phone unattended for several hours and truly unplug?

3. DRAW NEAR TO GOD. God can give you rest when you unburden yourself and your cares by drawing near to Him. He rewards a faithful heart who looks to Him for His rest. Let Him know that is why you are drawing near to Him and ask Him to cover you with His calming presence.

Schedule some time this week to be alone with God for an hour. You'll be impressed by how helpful that time is.

Rest is essential in allowing you to have the emotional and spiritual bandwidth to navigate seasons of loss and struggle. Look for ways to incorporate more rest into your life as you discover the benefit of God's provision of His peace when you seek Him.

Bible Study 1

THE LUXURY OF REST

Two men entered a competition to see who could cut down the most trees in a day. One of the men was much older and by looking at the two men, you would assume the younger man would win without much of a battle at all. He had youth on his side. He had strength on his side. It didn't appear to even be a question as to how this competition would wind up.

But every hour or so as they were chopping trees, the older man would go get a drink of water and sit down. He would sit there for about ten minutes and rest. The younger man kept chopping down trees, believing the prize money was his.

At the end of the day, the older man had chopped down twice as many trees as the younger guy. The younger man said, "I don't understand! You kept stopping to rest. How on earth did you chop down twice as much as me?" To which the older man replied, "Every time I took my break, I was sharpening my ax."

When you've got the right tool, you can afford to take a rest. You can sit down for a while. When you take Jesus' yoke upon you so that He can carry the burden of the hurt and pain you have been carrying for so long, you can relax. You can go further. You can last longer. You can contribute more.

Read the following Bible verses, summarizing the passage and writing down a personal application action item you learn from each one:

"Come to Me, all who are weary and burdened, and I will give you rest. Take My yoke upon you and learn from Me, for I am gentle and humble in heart, and YOU WILL FIND REST FOR YOUR SOULS. For My yoke is comfortable, and My burden is light."
MATTHEW 11:28-30

Summary:

Application:

And He said to them, "Come away by yourselves to a secluded
place and rest a little while." (For there were many people
coming and going, and they did not even have time to eat.)
MARK 6:31

Summary:

Application:

Cease striving and know that I am God;
I will be exalted among the nations,
I will be exalted in the earth.
PSALM 46:10

Summary:

Application:

Thus says the LORD, "Stand by the ways and see and ask for the
ancient paths, where the good way is, and walk in it; and you will
find rest for your souls." But they said, "We will not walk in it."
JEREMIAH 6:16

Summary:

Application:

Therefore humble yourselves under the mighty hand of God,
so that He may exalt you at the proper time, having cast
all your anxiety on Him, because He cares about you.
1 PETER 5:6-7

Summary:

Application :

Jesus offers us rest. But rest does not mean we will no longer have any issues to contend with. Too many people confuse the rest that Jesus offers with leisure and ease. The rest that Jesus offers refers to things such as peace, contentment, coping skills, and more. Jesus offers a rest for your soul, not a life of ease for your body.

What is the difference between spiritual rest and physical ease?

In what ways do we confuse the rest that Jesus has to offer with worldly ideas such as prosperity, abundance, and a problem-free life?

I was going through the airport on my way to a flight one day when I had suitcases in both hands. As they were starting to get heavy someone pointed out to me that they had wheels on the bottom. I had forgotten, but as soon as I put them down and pulled out the handled to roll them, my burden became light. The weight hadn't changed. Rather, how I interacted with the weight and the bags changed, and my burden eased. What once had caused me to sweat and struggle, now glided easily along the floor. The wheels enabled me to handle the weight they contained in an easier way.

Jesus' promise in Matthew 11:28-30 isn't a promise that you won't have any problems. He doesn't promise a world of peace or prosperity. But He does promise that how you feel it will be very different. How you interact with the burden and the weight will be very different. How far you can go while still having it will be very different. You won't get tired out from the load you have gotten in this life. Jesus promises you rest for your soul.

And we all need rest for our souls in a world where there's a list of things to worry about even before you even open your eyes in the morning.

What are some common worries and stresses that people deal with?

What are some ways Jesus gives us rest for our souls in the middle of facing life's struggles?

When have you experienced Jesus' rest during a difficult time?. What did you learn during that season?

Rest is becoming more and more of a luxury for people. Despite having more time on our hands, anxiety and stress are skyrocketing. The kind of rest Jesus offers means calm, peace, and internal stability during the storms of life.

Notice in Matthew 11 that Jesus changes how He talks about rest. At the start of the passage, He says He will "give" you rest. But then toward the end, He changes it a bit by saying "you will find rest." That's a different statement. Jesus can do both. He can give you rest and you can find rest. If you come to Him, He will give it to you at some level. But until you take His yoke and learn from Him and follow His ways based on what you learned; He will help you to locate the additional rest for those who pursue Him. You'll get a greater grace. You'll receive a personal peace. You'll experience an increased intimacy with the Source of rest itself. And couldn't we all use a bit more of rest right now?

PRAYER

Pray about your levels of rest, peace, calm, assurance, and intimacy with Jesus Christ. Ask God to reveal to you the ways in which you can manage your emotions underneath the overarching truth of His Word. Keep your eyes and heart open to what God is trying to teach you through this Bible study, and be sure to apply what you are learning.

YOUR FOCUS SETS YOU FREE

One of Satan's primary methods for getting a follower of Christ off the path he or she needs to be on is through emotional strongholds of pain, hurt, or sadness. When someone experiences pain in his or her life, it often leads to more pain because it starts a cycle of defeat in the mind. Or it lights a fire of blame in the spirit. There are a number of ways that Satan uses other people's wrong-doings against you in order to initiate a loop of self-sabotage down the road.

Jesus knows we need to be set free. That is why He has told us how to be free. He has asked us to receive spiritual freedom souls by simply coming to Him. Drawing near to Him. And taking His yoke upon us.

Jesus' might is the source of our own strength and His power and His grace fortify our souls with a confident rest. When we experience the grace of Christ Jesus, we learn how to give ourselves grace for the sins and mistakes of the past, and how to forgive others as well. When we refuse to come to Christ, we become trapped in Satan's web of lies.

Satan is a master at planting defeat and stress in your mind and having you replicate cycles of unease. Thoughts of low self-esteem, insignificance, and fear are his specialties. Some of his favorites might sound like this:

> *"I won't ever earn enough money to get ahead."*
> *"I could never compete against the others I work with for that promotion."*
> *"I can't let go of this pain in my heart that keeps me up at night."*

Those are some examples of the lies Satan tries to trap you in. He tries to make you weary as you battle these mental games in your head. Before you know it, you are exhausted from worry, regret, blame, and fear. But the truth of God's Word offers you life. It offers you the ability to get up from where you've been knocked down, and renew your strength as you yoke yourself with Jesus Christ.

Read God's promise through the prophet Isaiah.

Do you not know? Have you not heard?
The Everlasting God, the LORD, the Creator of the ends of the earth
Does not become weary or tired.
His understanding is unsearchable.
He gives strength to the weary,
And to the one who lacks might He increases power.
Though youths grow weary and tired,
And vigorous young men stumble badly,
Yet those who wait for the LORD
Will gain new strength;
They will mount up with wings like eagles,
They will run and not get tired,
They will walk and not become weary.
ISAIAH 40:28-31

List some of the lies or worries that make you weary.

Why is it important to let go of worries and fears that drain your energy?

Check any of the following that leave you feeling negative or tired:

☐ **browsing social media**
☐ **watching certain television shows**
☐ **eating certain foods**
☐ **engaging in an unhealthy relationship**
☐ **Other:_____**

If these things exhaust or strain you, why do we continue in them?

Write down some things, or even relationships, you may need to limit in order to renew your energy more so in the Lord.

We all know by now how important it is to renew and recharge the battery on our phones. If your phone does not abide with its charger long enough, it will have no power. When the Lord tells us to renew our strength on Him, He is letting us know where we go to regain power and remain charged. However, many of us give all our available time to things that drain us.

When troubling emotions, misguided activities, or toxic people and relationships give you a low-battery alert on life, you need to get connected to Christ in a closer way. These things weren't designed to give you strength. Jesus is the source of your strength. We gain power by connecting ourselves to Him. When we connect ourselves to His strength, we will mount up with wings like eagles, run and not get tired, and walk and not become weary. How we spend our time shapes our lives.

Read 1 Peter 5:8.

> Be of sober spirit, be on the alert. Your adversary, the devil,
> prowls around like a roaring lion, seeking someone to devour.
> **1 PETER 5:8**

In what ways does the devil seek to devour a person's strength, focus, passion or positive energy?

How does staying on the alert toward the devil's schemes help you to avoid them?

What are some ways to abide in Christ so that your energy can be renewed like the eagle?

When you abide in Jesus by taking His "yoke" upon you as we saw in the earlier passage, you will be positioning yourself to learn from Him. In learning from Him, you will discover how Jesus responds to circumstances that might fill us with fear or worry and the like. You will witness how Jesus responds when life gives Him a burden to bear. And as you get to know Him better, you will tap into what His Spirit says to your soul when you have an opportunity to respond to a difficulty yourself. If you choose to apply what you learn from Jesus to your emotions and actions, you will find hope for any hurt that you face.

Jesus wants you to learn from Him on how He is gentle and humble in heart. He wants you to not simply admire that He is gentle and humble in heart. He wants you to learn how to be gentle and humble in heart too. That's the key. It is in gentleness and humility that you will find rest for your soul.

If you learn from Jesus on how to respond to life's challenges through a gentleness, grace, and humility that reflects God's heart of love, you will become free from the trap of emotional bondage that keeps you from living for the glory of God and the good of others.

PRAYER

Jesus, I want to abide in You and receive the strength, lessons in humility and gentleness, and grace that comes from knowing You more fully. I want You alone to dominate my emotions so that I am no longer a slave to this world's agenda. Show me when I get off-track in my thoughts and actions so that I can stop them, and return to a focus on You which truly sets me free. In Your name, amen.

Week 6

TURNING BITTER
TO SWEET

Start

Welcome to Group Session 6.

What is one big lesson you took away from last session's focus on rest?

In this final session, we're going to focus on how God can take our bitter circumstances and turn them into evidence of His work in our lives that we can grow from. Hopefully, you've seen this throughout the study, but in this session, we're going to really press in.

What are some things in life that cause a bitter taste in a person's experience?

Does complaining about our experience improve them, or perpetuate them? Explain your answer.

As we near the end of our Bible study, be encouraged. Talking about our pain is not easy and takes commitment. Sticking with the process.

As we close out our time together in this last session, consider your role in finding hope in the midst of your hurt. How we respond to life's painful situations can contribute to our healing or stall it. Far too many of us want Jesus to swoop in and simply turn our hearts and lives around, but life is a participatory process. You must choose to receive God's help.

Invite someone to pray, then watch the video teaching.

Watch

Follow along as you watch video session 6.

Discuss

Use the following questions to discuss the video teaching.

How well did you do on tests in school?
What would you say is the purpose in taking a test?

Tests are common in school. Teachers give tests in order to identify whether or not we understood what we were taught. A person can say that they understand. They can even repeat back the words that have been spoken to them. But true understanding is revealed through a test.

What are some ways that God tests our faith in order to grow it?
When have you been through such a test?

Occasionally, God tests us as well. He will allow things to come into our lives to see whether or not what we say we believe is what we truly believe. No one enjoys going through a test, but they are a necessary part of demonstrating growth in grace and spiritual maturity.

Far too frequently, spiritual tests do come about through seasons of loss and struggle. There is something about the fire of pain that burns away any excess to reveal what is truly at the core of someone spiritually. These times not only help God to see whether or not you can pass the test, but they are also designed to help you. They are designed to help you see where you are, what you desire, and to even clarify what matters most to you. Be open to learning through these times rather than complaining. There is a lot you can learn through loss.

Why do you think people learn better during difficult times or challenging seasons?

What goals, desires, and sense of purposes has God clarified through pain He has allowed you to experience?

Is there someone you have watched who has learned well through loss? You may know them personally or even from afar. If so, what are some things you have learned through how they have responded in the midst of personal pain?

How do you know when you have not passed the test of the wilderness? Because you switch from thanksgiving to grumbling. Grumbling, or complaining, is a sure sign that you have not grown spiritually. Spiritual maturity means understanding and surrendering to God's sovereignty and aligning your life and whatever outcome that may entail. Spiritually mature people know that God is working all things together for good.

Why is it easier to complain than give thanks in the midst of pain?

What measures can you put in place to help shift your focus to a greater level of giving thanks rather than complaining?

PRAYER

Lord, we want to pass the tests You allow in our lives. We do not want to have to repeat them. Give us the spiritual maturity and strength to get through them in a way that demonstrates personal, emotional, and spiritual maturity. Remind us that our lives are a lesson in learning how to reflect You more fully and represent Jesus Christ in all I do. Help me to grow, God. In Jesus' name, amen.

Hit the Streets

SWEET AND SOUR

Sometimes life can get pretty sour. It can leave you wishing for something sweet to get rid of the bitter taste in your mouth. We all face these trying times. We have all taken a bite out of a challenging moment only to want to spit it back out. Moses was instructed to throw a branch from a tree into the water to make it sweet again. Now, the branch didn't contain any special forces for cleaning the toxic water. But what it did contain was faith. Moses was called to exhibit faith, and when he did, God acted.

There are times in your life when God is going to ask you to do something that doesn't make sense. He's going to give you the direction you are needing but you might scratch your head when you hear it. Wouldn't it be great to know what Moses was thinking when he held that branch? Do you wonder if he questioned whether or not he grabbed the right one? Yet Moses responded in faith to what God said because Moses knew that while God doesn't always make sense, He does make miracles.

Miracles are when God steps in to fix an unfixable situation. Miracles come in all shapes and sizes, like a branch being tossed into the water. But one of the common features of miracles in the Bible is that they always started out with a requirement. It took faith on the part of the person who needed the miracle. Faith is critical to receiving the healing you need to experience in life's difficult times. Let's examine three ways to strengthen your faith so when the time calls for it, you can obey God by doing whatever He asks you to do.

1. STUDY THE SCRIPTURE and examples of people who stepped out in faith. Write down any correlations you find between them, or between what they did.

What examples come to mind?

2. ASK GOD TO GIVE YOU SMALL STEPS to take which demonstrate faith so you can experience success in exercising your faith muscles.

> **When has God asked you to do something that didn't make sense? What as the result?**

3. ASK GOD FOR MORE FAITH. There is a man in Scripture who knew he did not have enough faith. So he asked Jesus to give him more (see Mark 9:24). Make the prayer for increased faith part of your everyday prayer journey.

> **End your time today praying for God to increase your faith.**

Growing your faith is part of the process of learning to navigate seasons of loss. The greater your faith, the greater your ability to experience the sweetness of God in the midst of the bitterness life brings your way.

Bible Study 1

PRAISING IN THE PAIN

Throughout the Old Testament, God continually reminds His people that He was the One who delivered them. He reminded them so that when they ran into a new problem, hurt, or disappointment, they would remember their God who is bigger than any obstacle the faced.

When life gets bitter or your heart gets hurt, it's easy to forget what God did yesterday. Now, I'm not saying that we should always be focusing on the past. Rather, we should remember the faithfulness of God to us.

How has God healed your hurt in the past?

What lessons did you learn from the times God has provided you healing?

How can we learn from the past without living in the past?

God wants us to remember those times when He healed, delivered, or redeemed us from a heart of regret, blame, or brokenness. He wants us to remember His strength and recall how He is able to turn things around. We must actively remind ourselves that the same God who showed up back then can show up right now. He is able. But when we give in to hopeless thoughts and complaining, we are doing a disservice to God's former work in our lives and the things He has taught us.

Read Exodus 15:19-24.

For the horses of Pharaoh with his chariots and his horsemen went into the sea, and the LORD brought back the waters of the sea on them, but the sons of Israel walked on dry land through the midst of the sea. Miriam the prophetess, Aaron's sister, took the tambourine in her hand, and all the women went out after her with tambourines and with dancing. And Miriam answered them, "Sing to the LORD, for He is highly exalted; The horse and his rider He has hurled into the sea." Then Moses led Israel from the Red Sea, and they went out into the wilderness of Shur; and they went three days in the wilderness and found no water. When they came to Marah, they could not drink the waters of Marah, because they were bitter; for that reason it was named Marah. So the people grumbled at Moses, saying, "What are we to drink?"

EXODUS 15:19-24

What was challenging Israel in this moment? What had just occurred?

What can cause a person to go from praise to grumbling?

How could the Israelites have benefited by remembering that God had recently led them through the Red Sea?

The Israelites went from praising to complaining as fast as possible. They went from thanking God for opening the waters and allowing them to pass through. to grumbling at God for leading them to water that was bitter. It's almost as if they started complaining once they hit the parking lot after church. Has that ever happened to you? You feel the fullness of the Spirit and the joy of the Lord during a worship service only to reach your car and get upset with the driver in front of you who stops too quickly or cuts in. Our emotions can go from high to low a lot faster than most of us prefer, or would like to admit. Which is exactly what happened to the Israelites, as we see in the passage above.

How would you define the difference between a conditional praise and a faith-filled praise?

In what ways does faith-filled praise, in the midst of life's difficulties, honor God's rightful place in our lives and hearts?

Faith-filled praise relies on us choosing to remember God's past actions and deliverance on our behalf. I understand that sometimes what we are going through can suck us dry of any hope for tomorrow. In fact, it can suck us so dry that we forget that while circumstances may change, God does not. The Israelites were on a new journey of faith with Yaweh, and they had already forgotten an important truth.

Once they found the bitter water could not satisfy their thirst, they complained. They argued. They grumbled. In essence, they went to their leader, Moses, and demanded he do something or take them back to Egypt. This was not the freedom they were hoping for. So, Moses went from praise to problem to prayer. Notice how Moses responded.

> Then he cried out to the LORD, and the LORD showed him a tree;
> and he threw it into the waters, and the waters became sweet.
> **EXODUS 15:25**

Describe the difference between "crying out to the Lord" and "routine prayer."

Have you ever "cried out to the Lord," and if so, what was the result?

Whenever the Bible talks about "crying out," it's not referring to a simple prayer. To cry out to God implies that you are desperate, your situation is serious, and you need Him to intervene. Moses has an enormous, tired crowd under his charge who were thirsty. But the water they found was undrinkable. Moses faced the potential of having the people he just led to freedom die from dehydration. Of course he cried out. He didn't settle for routine prayer.

When Moses cried out—God showed him His plan.

Keep in mind, God did not show him the solution until he cried out. Also keep in mind, the solution seemed—weird. But isn't that how God can work at times? I know most pastors won't openly call God's ways weird, but if we were honest, who would have thought that holding up a stick would cause a sea to divide? Who would have thought that tossing a stick into bitter water would make it sweet? Those are new strategies to most of us. Some might even consider them strange. Which is why it's critical that as you work through the healing of life's hurts, you stick close to God. His plan to make the bitter waters you may be tasting turn to sweet won't be the same plan for everyone else. And it probably won't be a plan you would have thought up on your own.

It is in staying near to God and crying out to Him rather than complaining to others that you will hear the pathway to experiencing relief and enjoying peace.

Have you ever had to trust a plan given to you by God that seemed "weird"? If so, what was the result? If not, can you share what you learned from a biblical event where God's ways seemed "weird?"

PRAYER

Pray and ask God to show you His plans for healing your heart. Ask Him to show you what you need to do in order to regain the wholeness and peace you once felt, or want to feel. Dedicate time to spending in His Word or alone with Him in prayer, seeking His direction for your life. Surrender your own attempts at solving life's issues. Surrender them over to God and let Him know You will follow Him based on how He leads you.

Bible Study 2

YOU GET TO CHOOSE

When God placed humanity on earth, He gave us the gift of free will. God did not create robots to rule over. He provided each of us with the opportunity, and responsibility, to choose what we think, say, and do with our lives.

Free will affords us many options. We can use our freedom for good or for ill. However, as we sow, we will also reap.

What are some of the benefits of being able to make choices?

What are some consequences that come from making the wrong choices?

Read Deuteronomy 30:19-20.

I call heaven and earth to witness against you today, that
I have placed before you life and death, the blessing and the
curse. So choose life in order that you may live, you and your
descendants, by loving the LORD your God, by obeying His voice,
and by holding close to Him; for this is your life and the length of
your days, that you may live in the land which the LORD swore
to your fathers, to Abraham, Isaac, and Jacob, to give them.
DEUTERONOMY 30:19-20

What are some things this passage describes which exemplify "choosing life?"

Free will means that every person is afforded with choices. We get to choose the actions we make, thoughts we think, and words we say—all of which come with consequences built in.

How do the choices we make when faced with hurt make our situation better or worse?

God has set before each of us the free will to choose. We can complain. He's given us that option. We can give up. He's also given us that option. We can throw in the towel. God is not going to force anyone to believe in Him, or to act like it either. But when you make those choices and fail to throw the tree into the bitter water because you would rather complain at how bitter the water has become, then don't blame God when the water remains bitter. God will receive our response, but we must be aware that we have a choice.

God gets far more blame for things that we do and we create than He ever could deserve. Often the hurt surrounding our circumstances are beyond our control, however we remain hurt because we fail to help ourselves. God is willing to help us turn our bitter to sweet as we depend upon Him. Our circumstances may not change, but out outlook on them and out attitude in dealing with them will. We have the power to see God's power in our weakness. When that happens we see learn about God's good character.

What are some ways we side-step choosing God and His hand in delivering us?

Why do you think it's important not to distract yourself from life's painful situations but rather to embrace those seasons in life and learn from them?

The only time you truly know the value and strength of an anchor is in a storm. It is when the waters around you are causing you to shake to the point that you can no longer stand on your own. That's when you see God show up. In fact, nothing will make God more real to you than the bitterness you feel. Nothing will make God more real to you than those times when what you thought was a blessing turns bitter. Maybe it's a job that has turned bitter, or a marriage, or a friendship any number of things.

When things get bitter, your view of God gets bigger than ever before—if and when you cry out to Him and then do what He says to do. God is often doing His greatest work when He is nowhere to be found. God does some of His best work in the dark. In those times when you don't think He is doing a thing, He's up to something great behind the scenes. But He's waiting for you to call out to Him so He can reveal to you His pathway for you to sweeter waters.

God longs to bring you and me into deeper relationship with Him. He does this because He knows that it is in those seasons of struggle that we learn how strong He truly is. He wants to take the Bible off of the pages of paper and put it into the fabric of our lives. You may know the Word of God but He wants you to experience the words of God speaking to your spirit right now. He speaks to you through His Spirit.

How do you discern it is the Holy Spirit speaking to you as opposed to your own thoughts?

Why is it important to place what you feel the Spirit is telling you against the backdrop of God's revealed Word?

We are all on a journey of maturing spiritually from the hurts we experience in life. Sometimes God uses our hurt get our attention and our focus, or help us prioritize what we really want in life. There are numerous reasons why God allows pain. But rather than complain, we need to remind ourselves that there is a purpose for this journey and a good plan up ahead.

The temptation to complain, blame, and grumble when things don't go our way is there for each of us. But it is in those times that it is most important to hold on to God like never before. Wrap your heart around His hope with a faith that you have never shown before. There are times in your life when faith will be all you have. These dark nights in our lives look like even God has backed away and things are regressing.

But God reminds us through the stories we have looked at in this Bible study together that it is in those times that He wants us to embrace His statues, ordinances, and commands the most. He wants you to reach out and embrace Him and His Word, His will and His kingdom agenda. He wants you to discover for yourself that He truly can turn the bitter into something sweet.

Where are you hoping to see God turn from bitter into sweet? Pray for those things as we close our study.

PRAYER

Let's close our time together in this Bible study with prayer. Heavenly Father, thank You for the power of Your Word. Thank You for the intimacy that comes in abiding with Jesus Christ. Thank You for the revelation You give through the speaking of the Spirit into my life. I know that You have a good plan for me and that You will reveal this over time. I look to You to heal my hurt and use the pain that has come into my life as a platform for greater authenticity, hope and peace within my soul. In Christ's name, amen.

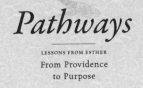

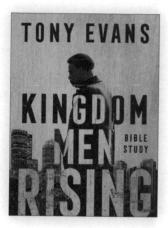

KINGDOM MEN RISING
Heaven's Representatives on Earth

Discover the biblical truth about the purpose and future of masculinity, and inspire your group to fulfill God's intent. (6 sessions)

Bible Study Kit $99.99
Bible Study Book $14.99

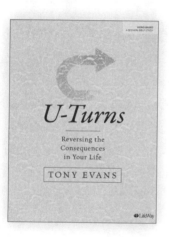

U-TURNS
Reversing the Consequences in Your Life

Learn to align your life choices under God's Word and change the direction of your life. (6 sessions)

Bible Study Kit $99.99
Bible Study Book $14.99

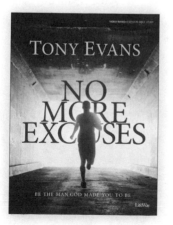

NO MORE EXCUSES
Be the Man God Made You to Be

Learn to lay down your excuses, stop compromising, and fight to be a man of character and commitment. (8 sessions)

Bible Study Kit $99.99
Bible Study Book $14.99

Prices and availability subject to change without notice.

YOUR *Eternity* IS OUR *Priority*

At The Urban Alternative, eternity is our priority—for the individual, the family, the church and the nation. The 45-year teaching ministry of Tony Evans has allowed us to reach a world in need with:

The Alternative – Our flagship radio program brings hope and comfort to an audience of millions on over 1,300 radio outlets across the country.

tonyevans.org – Our library of teaching resources provides solid Bible teaching through the inspirational books and sermons of Tony Evans.

Tony Evans Training Center – Experience the adventure of God's Word with our online classroom, providing at-your-own-pace courses for your PC or mobile device.

Tony Evans app – Packed with audio and video clips, devotionals, Scripture readings and dozens of other tools, the mobile app provides inspiration on-the-go.

**Explore God's kingdom today.
Live for more than the moment.
Live for *eternity*.**

tonyevans.org